THE
VERY BEST OF BRITISH

Second in the Series

by

Richard Danielson
and
John Hendy

FERRY
Publications

ISBN 0 9513155 3 6
© Richard Danielson and John Hendy 1991

Published by Ferry Publications at P.O. Box 1, Laxey, Isle of Man.
Text origination by The DeskTop Publishing Service, Douglas
Printed by Eyre & Spottiswoode Ltd, London and Margate

(Front cover) *The* **Lord of the Isles** *sweeps into Oban Bay between the island of Kerrera and Maiden Island. Photo: Walter Bowie.*

(Inside front cover) *The* **Lord Warden** *arriving at Boulogne on 13th September 1975.*   *Photo: Andrew Jones.*

(Inside back cover) *The* **Balmoral** *scudding into Peel, (population 3,660) Cathedral City of the Isle of Man in glorious, if lively, coastal cruising weather.*
          Photo: Richard Danielson.

(Back cover) *The ever-lasting* **Balmoral** *takes the Irish Sea in her stride.*
          Photo: Richard Danielson.

Caledonian MacBrayne
Hebridean and Clyde Ferries

The production of even a small book like this, the second in its series, with high definition black and white scanned monochromes and a plethora of colour photographs is very expensive. Without the support of a major shipping operator it would be impossible to contemplate such a costly exercise, if it were to cater solely for the lover of ferries, cross- channel boats and excursion ships. Therefore, the authors would like to place on record their appreciation of the help and encouragement they have received from Caledonian MacBrayne Limited, who, directly and through its predecessors have, for more than a century, provided the Clyde and Scotland's Western Isles with its premier shipping service. There is no doubt that many of their ships have been and remain amongst the finest in their class and, in time to come, more will rightfully earn the accolade — "The Very Best of British".

CONTENTS

Few ships attain an active lifespan of over forty years but in this 1968 view of the **Balmoral** *off Worthing, she was already almost twenty years old and coming to the end of her career with Red Funnel. Who ever would have guessed the exciting future that lay before her? Photo: David Parsons.*

T.S.M.V. **BALMORAL**

Built: 1949 Builder: J I Thornycroft, Woolston, Southampton. Speed: 14 knots
Dimensions: 203' x 32'   Gross tonnage: 688 tons as built, 736 tons after 1986 rebuild.
Machinery: 2 x Newbury Sirron diesels, total 1,200bhp.
Owner/Operator: Southampton, Isle of Wight & South of England Royal Mail
Steam Packet Company Limited (Red Funnel Services) 1949/1969
P. & A. Campbell Limited 1969/1982
Craig Inns, Dundee 1982/1985
Balmoral Excursions Limited 1985 to date.

The shipping route to the Isle of Wight from Southampton has, since 1861, been in the capable hands of operators regaled with the longest name of all known shipping companies — The Southampton, Isle of Wight & South of England Royal Mail Steam Packet Company Limited. Understandably, they trade under the more manageable banner of Red Funnel and were, until taken over in October 1989 by Associated British Ports (owners of Southampton Docks) a publicly quoted, independent group of companies. Their principal business includes the carriage of passengers, cars and freight by sea to and from Cowes, Isle of Wight, and the operation of a modern fleet of tugs. They continue to have an interest in Cosens and Co., former operators of paddle excursion steamers and marine engineers but now involved only in general engineering at Portland. They used also to operate tenders for visiting ocean liners and variety of pleasure trips and excursions in and around the Solent and South Coast. Trips across the English Channel were also offered until the outbreak of World War 2. Except for odd sorties by car ferries later, the excursion business ceased altogether in 1968, when the **Balmoral**, the subject of this story and the last conventional passenger ferry in the service of the Company, was withdrawn.

When Mrs C D Pinnock, wife of the then Chairman of the Company launched the ship on 27th June 1949, it is hard to imagine that she was contemplating the long term future of the **Balmoral** and what might become of "her" ship more than forty years on. Indeed, she would have needed to be farsighted in the extreme to know what a superb, versatile and long lived vessel, the ship she was sponsoring, was to become.

Despite the somewhat private yacht-like appearance and lines, lovingly ascribed to her by many, (Thornycroft being renowned for the building of several such craft) by design, the **Balmoral** was to be anything but glamorous in operation. Winter and summer, her principal duty was to be on the Company's service route from Southampton to Cowes, on the Isle of Wight. In summer (less in winter), she carried up to 892 passengers, or 712 passengers plus about 10 cars and items of cargo on her mostly open car deck aft, which was specially strengthened for the purpose. Carrying the mail was an important part of her business too and it was locked in a special mail room, forward on the main deck. For these tasks she was eminently suitable and was clearly a great improvement on her predecessors, although perhaps, she lacked the charisma of her paddle driven, older consorts. Principally, she was to be an utterly dependable workhorse capable of sustained and at times intense, operations. Although she arrived towards the end of an older era, for most of her career on the Isle of Wight service, she will be remembered running alongside the Company's other motorships, **Medina, Vecta, Norris Castle** and the paddle steamers **Princess Elizabeth** and **Bournemouth Queen**. In addition to the service packet route, the **Balmoral** was also designed to be able to act as tender to visiting ocean liners during which, passengers' cars for shipment, trunks and other bulky items would be lifted aloft onto the liner by derrick.

In 1950, 1951 and 1952 the Southampton Company took out of service, four old vessels that they had purchased to replenish their fleet after the War, and they were disposed of permanently. These were the ageing **Robina**, previously a veritable nomad that they had acquired in 1948, the former Mersey ferry **Upton** also acquired in 1948 and the two Naval paddle minesweepers that they had acquired in 1949 and

renamed **Lorna Doone** and **Solent Queen.** As a result of the departure of the last two in particular, our ship, the brand new **Balmoral**, was to take on her third important role - as an excursion ship.

The **Balmoral** has always had an excellent turn of speed and this rendered her particularly suitable for long cruises, especially those round the Isle of Wight. Another good money spinner for the Company at that time were dock cruises to view the liners and the **Balmoral** took her share of these, especially when the paddlers were otherwise employed. Two years before the **Balmoral** had entered service, the Red Funnel company had purchased a 1942 vintage, tank landing craft which, very successfully, they reconstructed as a passenger, freight and vehicle carrier. Renamed **Norris Castle,** that vessel operated for twenty years and was joined

*The **Balmoral** will always be remembered for her sailings up the River Avon whose tortuous, winding course has caused many an anxious moment for Masters of Bristol-bound ships. These two views show the **Balmoral** on a rare charter cruise from the City Docks. Photos: Richard Danielson.*

On 27th September 1967, the Cunard liner **Queen Mary** arrives at Southampton from New York for the very last time. The **Balmoral** and the **Hotspur IV** (the latter en route to Hythe) are both doing good business, witnessing the sad event. Photo: John Hendy.

Acting as tender to the **Kungsholm** *at Douglas. Photo: Richard Danielson*

The popular, annual White Funnel trips, west from the Bristol Channel out into the Atlantic and on to the Isles of Scilly, sometimes included a call at St. Ives on Cornwall's northern coast. It was also a convenient harbour in which to find shelter when the need arose. The **Balmoral** *is seen at St. Ives on 16th October 1977. Photo: Gordon Ditchfield.*

The **Balmoral** in dry-dock at Dundee, on 17th March 1985, about to become consort to the legendary paddle steamer, **Waverley**.
Photo: Joe McKendrick.

by the purpose-built vehicle ferries **Carisbrooke Castle** (1959) and the **Osborne Castle** (1962) immediately after which the old **Norris Castle** was withdrawn.

At about this time, two important acts were taking place in the coastal passenger ship scene. P & A Campbell Limited, the Bristol based operator of the famous White Funnel Fleet had been having a tough time and, having gone into Receivership in 1959 looked unlikely to recover. At the other end of the country and previously quite unconnected, the now much lamented Liverpool & North Wales Steamship Company Limited were in the final throws of corporate demise. The end was perilously close for them and whilst for the North Wales Company there was to be no turning back, mercifully, things were different for Campbells. Their financial position brought them close to the perspicacious Chartered Accountant, Mr S Clifton Smith-Cox whose undoubted financial ability combined with a flair for the steamers, were responsible for their recovery and modest success throughout the next almost thirty years. He had had a lifelong interest in Bristol Channel pleasure steamers and when in 1952 he had been invited to join the Campbell's board of directors he did so, probably knowing that the road ahead would be tough. He became Joint Managing Director in 1954, sole Managing Director a year later and Chairman too, shortly thereafter.

He negotiated with the Company's bankers and with George Nott Industries Limited and in the end, P & A Campbell Limited's survival became possible.

The success of his rescue package was based upon the Company being taken over by George Nott Industries Limited who owned the potentially powerful Townsend Bros. Car Ferries and for Campbell's past losses to be available to offset, for tax purposes, against the profits of the burgeoning Townsend operation.

In the event, the two ageing North Wales steamships were scrapped and the Company was wound up but, in February 1963, their one motorship, the diminutive and very economic **St. Trillo** (1936), was sold to Townsend Bros. Car Ferries for use by their newly acquired, loss-making subsidiary, P & A Campbell Limited, for further service both in North Wales and in the Bristol Channel. For Campbells, this event marked a turning point in their fortunes.

Back at Southampton, the passenger ship **Vecta** carried on in company with the **Balmoral** until 1965, by which time Red Funnel had taken delivery of its third purpose-built vehicle ferry, the **Cowes Castle.** In September 1965 the **Vecta**, being surplus to Red Funnel's needs, was sold to Townsend Bros. Car Ferries Limited and, complete with her Southampton Company red funnel, was immediately used by P & A Campbell Limited for the last few weeks of the excursion season in the Bristol Channel area. Shortly thereafter, she was renamed **Westward Ho** and repainted in the Campbell livery. Campbell's famous paddle steamers, the **Cardiff Queen** and the **Bristol Queen** were withdrawn after the 1966 and 1967 seasons respectively.

It was not until 1968, with the expected arrival of the fourth purpose built car ferry (this one giving new life to the name **Norris Castle**), that the **Balmoral** was unceremoniously withdrawn. It had been planned to run a farewell trip on 15th September 1968 but nature intervened on the day with floods of rain and the trip was scrubbed!

The **Balmoral** was put on the sale list and aroused the interest of P & A Campbell Limited, just as the **Vecta** had previously. She was duly taken on charter for the 1969 summer season and, having surrendered her red and black distinctive, flat-topped funnel in favour of the all white Campbell version, she immediately went into service in the Bristol Channel.

In an attempt to make the ship more manageable in the much rougher seas of the Bristol Channel, especially the lower reaches, during her first season she carried various

In this 1969 photograph, her first season on the Bristol Channel, the **Balmoral** *(not yet sporting the traditional cowl top to her newly painted white funnel) is seen going astern from the Birnbeck Pier at Weston. Campbells owned the pier until 1972.* Photo: Richard Danielson

weights aft, on what had been her car deck. The weights were replaced with permanent ballast tanks once the secret had been discovered.

In the absence of vehicles, this deck became a popular venue for enthusiastic, regular supporters of the White Funnel Fleet, on which they would gather in small conclaves, notebooks at the ready and discuss the prospects for the day in minute detail. For others, it was a place to congregate for a while, have a cup of coffee, (or was it tea? to coin John Hendy's ancient quip) and to ponder the effort being expended by the ship's faithful Newbury Sirron diesels as the frothy, white wake churned out in an endless torrent, astern. It really was a most pleasant deck, providing plenty of sheltered space, normally free of funnel emissions and with plenty of sun (on the right day). Alternatively, in rough, following seas the full effect could best be experienced there, as could the less attractive odours of the muddy River Avon at low tide, on a warm summer's evening cruise up to Hotwells! Even by the lively standards of the **St. Trillo**, it was found that the **Balmoral** was quite capable of reducing even the most hardened sailor to pallor. Trips down-Channel to open water could prove very exciting, moving experiences and even on some end-of-season crossings from Weston to Penarth and Cardiff, the traveller was left wondering about the accuracy of the use of the word "pleasure" in conjunction with such boisterous trips. The majority of trips were, of course, completed in glorious, calm, summer seasonal weather but it is always the rough trips that attain notoriety.

After the end of the 1969 season, which she spent mainly on the North Wales run, the **St. Trillo** remained laid-up at Barry, until she was finally scrapped in Dublin, four years later. The **Westward Ho** was taken out of service with irreparable engine trouble in 1971 and was later sold for static use.

The **Balmoral** was then taken on demise charter for ten years as a result of which, she was finally transferred by Red Funnel to P & A Campbell Limited for a nominal sum in 1980. Throughout this period (and until 1985, in fact), she remained registered at Southampton, the seat of her former owners.

The **Balmoral** was therefore left as the likely sole heir to the once busy Campbell empire and it was perhaps surprising to find that in 1977, the **Scillonian** (II) was acquired and renamed **Devonia** (but after two brief periods of operations, was subsequently laid up) and later sold to become the **Devoniun** based at Torquay. The **Balmoral** really did then have to soldier on alone, enjoying a reputation of immortality by keeping alive the coastal cruising tradition whereas others, all around our shores, had failed.

*Britain's most widely travelled excursion "steamer". The **Balmoral** at (top right) Llandudno, (top left) Lundy Island, (bottom right) Raglan Pier, Port Erin, Isle of Man and (bottom left) with a full load at Douglas, Isle of Man.*

All photos: Richard Danielson.

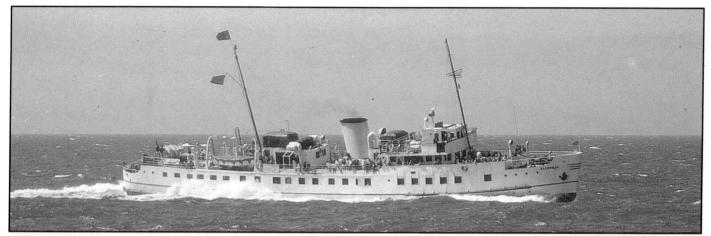

*In Manx waters on several occasions in June 1989 and 1990, the **Balmoral** displayed some of the lively characteristics for which she is renowned! All photos: Richard Danielson.*

Finally, the inevitable happened. The end came quite quickly in 1979 when Campbells announced that they were withdrawing from the excursion ship business. The following year, they "managed" the **Balmoral** on behalf of White Funnel Steamers Limited, set up by the Landmark Trust (Lundy) to whom they had chartered the ship. The arrangement did not extend beyond the end of the 1980 season — the final sailing being on 14th October.

The **Balmoral** was laid up first at Bristol and then she moved down to Avonmouth where it was thought she would be more accessible to prospective buyers and in March 1982 she was purchased by Craig Inns of Dundee for use as a floating public house and restaurant. She sailed north, via Land's End and the English Channel, under her own "steam"

N. Holman & Son Limited's dry-dock and ship repair business at Penzance was host to the **Balmoral** *on several occasions. She is seen here on a dull day during her March 1975 overhaul, having just vacated the dry-dock. She had spent the earlier part of that winter at Dartmouth, where Philip & Sons carried out essential main engine repairs. Photo: Richard Danielson.*

with one of her new owners' representatives, Captain Brian Macleod in command, but their plans proved to be unsuccessful and the whole venture was a sad failure, closing after just a few months.

At Dundee, the **Balmoral** languished, boarded up and deteriorating — at least superficially.

In March 1985 the **Waverley** organisation were looking for a new vessel to partner their legendary paddle steamer and they decided to acquire the **Balmoral** (from Craig Inns' bankers who were selling the ship as mortgagees in possession) with a view to raising funds to enable her to return to full operational use. After inspection and dry-docking at Dundee, the **Balmoral** was duly pronounced reasonably fit and well, particularly considering her long period of idleness. She set sail, north-about via the Pentland Firth and Cape Wrath, to begin her major rebuilding on the Clyde. Funds were raised by the Paddle Steamer Preservation Society and their many "friends" and much work was achieved whilst the ship was at Govan in the winter of 1985/86.

After trials and official testing by the Department of Transport, on 10th April 1986 the **Balmoral** left Glasgow bound for Bristol to begin her new career. She had emerged from that winter's work, a completely new looking ship. Perished steelwork had been cut away and replaced, as were the clinker built wooden lifeboats. The area towards the stern of the ship, once her car deck, had been completely plated-in to provide a large, if traditionally slightly spartan, full width cafeteria and galley. Space for the officers and crew to eat their meals was provided there too, but only separated from the travelling public by a rather flimsy curtain. Understandable maybe, but not very pretty, it brings to mind the story of the passenger on the famous Cunard liner, who, when his turn came to be afforded the ultimate accolade and was invited to dine at the Captain's table said, indignantly, that he had not paid all this money to eat with the crew!

Most striking of all, she had been repainted all white, with green boot-topping and a yellow funnel. Her publicity machine would now refer to her as "the motor yacht, *Balmoral*" but beneath her new "finery", to those of us who knew her, she was still the same delightful, seemingly ageless ship. In her interior, slightly dim lamps, barely illuminated the same bulkheads, dingy corners, cream painted alleyways and companionways. Lower still, in the bowels of the ship, the crew's quarters remained, but now they were to become a home for her men for months on end, when away. Thankfully, you could still stand abaft the funnel with its (just perceptible) warmth providing some respite from the numbing autumn gale, while listening to the diesel drone, rumbling away beneath you. Down below, the same old engines, one of which is taken apart each year for overhaul, still welcomed the inquisitive, with a tantalising mixture of noise, smell, polished metals and the inevitable springs and rockers pounding out their comforting message that all was well. Neither had her bare wooden decks (some heavily worn by the passage of time and millions of pairs of feet) greatly changed, save for the enthusiastic pourings from the deck-caulkers' tar buckets! It was good to have the old ship back.

Very early the next day, the *Balmoral* sailed south past the Isle of Man where, more than a decade previously (and several times before that) she had acted as tender to the Swedish liner, *Kungsholm*. Thus, she had finally circumnavigated the whole of the British mainland coastline, itself something of an achievement for an excursion ship licensed for "short excursions to sea".

Under the *Waverley* banner and the expert command of her master Captain Steve Michel, the *Balmoral* flourishes. Today, in a season that lasts from Easter through to the end of September, the *Balmoral* operates an extensive schedule of excursions all around the coast of the British Isles. Sadly, Lundy Island, once a regular destination for Campbell's ships and for the *Waverley* and *Balmoral* later, no longer allows them to call. The *Balmoral* visits nearly a hundred ports, harbours and piers a year and in 1990 alone, carried over 120,000 passengers! On sailings from Northern Ireland and Scotland she regularly visits the Isle of Man, once the remotest of her destinations and now one of the most popular! She operates on a Class III passenger certificate for 691 and on a Class IV, she can carry 800.

The *Balmoral*'s winter overhauls are usually spent at Bristol where she can dry-dock with comparative ease and where she can be reached by her precious volunteer labour force.

The *Balmoral*, now having attained the age of 42 years and her older fleetmate, the *Waverley*, must be the unchallengeable holders of the title "the world's most widely travelled excursion ships". Long may they continue!

The **Balmoral** at Weymouth on 1st May 1971 for a P.S.P.S. charter, with the **Caesarea** departing for the Channel Isles.   Photo: R. B. Adams

A rare trials view of the **Caesarea** *with the original application of her hull paint.* *Photo: John Hendy collection.*

During her first visit to Dover in winter 1966/67, the **Caesarea** *is seen leaving for Calais on the "Golden Arrow" service. Photo: John Hendy. (Right) A magnificent view of the* **Caesarea** *at speed. Photo: John Hendy collection.*

*The **Caesarea** at her home port of Weymouth bathed in warm afternoon sunlight.*　　　　　*Photo: Richard Danielson.*

T.S.S. **CAESAREA**

Built: 1960
Speed: 19.5 knots
Gross Tonnage: 4,174 tons until 1969, then 3,992 tons
Machinery: Twin screw, Pametrada double reduction, geared turbines, 8500 shp
Two Foster Wheeler water tube oil fired boilers
Owners/Operators:

Builders: J. Samuel White & Co., East Cowes, Isle of Wight
Dimensions: 322' x 51'

British Transport Commission 1960/1963
British Railways Board 1963/1969
British Rail (Shipping and International Services Division) 1969/1979
Sealink U.K. Ltd. 1979/1980
Apolina Ltd., Hong Kong 1980/1984
Philippines 1984/1986
Hiro Kisen K.K. Japan 1986

When the turbine steamer **Caesarea** tied-up at Folkestone on the evening of 4th October 1980, she not only brought to an end the 77 year history of the cross-Channel turbine powered passenger ship but also ended 159 years of steam driven passenger vessels across the Dover Strait.

The **Caesarea** and her twin sister **Sarnia** were products of the J. Samuel White yard at East Cowes, Isle of Wight. There was no cross-Channel ship expertise at the yard and other better-known builders of these highly specialist craft were overlooked in favour of a "local" concern to which the Southern Region's Marine Department had easy access. There is little doubt that White's produced two extremely fine steamers, representing as thy did, the final flowering of the traditional "steam packet". Even so, had they both been built a few years later, they would probably have been vastly different ships.

The traditional routes to the Channel Islands were the London & South Western Railway's link from Southampton and the rival Great Western route from Weymouth. The rivalry was so intense that races invariably developed, the most infamous of these ending in tragedy when in March

1899, the nine year old **Stella** ran onto the notorious Casquets, off Alderney, resulting in the loss of over one hundred lives.

In 1923, The Southern Railway Co. superseded the LSWR but the rivalry continued. The Great Western Railway went to John Brown's of Clydebank for its new **St. Julien** and **St. Helier** which entered service in 1925 while in 1930 the Southern countered with the **Isle of Jersey** and **Isle of Guernsey** from Denny's Dumbarton yard. Two years later they were joined by the **Isle of Sark.**

By the late fifties, there was growing criticism of the on-board standards experienced by passengers and it was decided to rationalise the service by withdrawing the longer Southampton route and introducing two new ships for the revamped Weymouth link. Not only were they to be larger than anything previously seen but they were also to be one class ships which would speed up the passage by not carrying cargo which had frequently delayed turn-round times. The names for the new twins were seen as a compromise, reviving as they did those of the old South Western sisters of 1910/11. Caesarea is the Roman name for Jersey while

Sarnia was Latin for Guernsey.

The **Caesarea** was launched into the River Medina by Lady Coutanche, wife of the Bailiff of Jersey, on 29th January 1960. At 322 feet in length, the new ship was said to be the largest which could enter the small Victorian harbour at St. Helier, Jersey, where the berthing procedure was always of great interest. On passing through the narrow pierheads, a hawser was passed ashore to starboard on which she would swing once the stern was safely inside the entrance. This pivoting movement swung the stern through 90 degrees after which the vessel would go astern up the Albert Harbour to her berth.

When launched, the **Caesarea**'s black hull paint ran in a straight line from her fo'c'sle to her poop and thus adorned she carried out her trials. The **Sarnia** too appeared on the stocks in this condition but neither ship saw service in it. During dry-docking at Southampton in September 1960, the **Caesarea** had her paint raised a deck higher, presumably to make her look less top-heavy.

Finally leaving Cowes on 5th November, the **Caesarea** sailed to Southampton and then to Weymouth where she was praised for her modern accommodation for 1400 passengers. She and her sister were fully stabilised, ensuring that sea travel to the Islands would be as comfortable as possible, even at the height of winter gales. Readers may recall that, back in 1936, the Southampton-based **Isle of Sark** with her rare maierform bow, was fitted experimentally with the original Denny-Brown gyro stabilisers.

A press trip from Southampton was given on 16th November and the **Caesarea**'s official maiden voyage was carried out on 2nd December when the ship replaced the former Great Western vessel **St. Patrick** (1948) which was sent to Cardiff for conversion to one class operations. Reappearing during the following April, the **St. Patrick** allowed the **Caesarea** to go off service for a pre-season refit. The new **Sarnia** appeared

on station on 17th June 1961 permitting the **St. Patrick** to stand back and be rostered for reliefs and excursions but when the **Caesarea** had to return to dry-dock to remedy vibration problems, the **St. Patrick** filled her place. Out of retirement came the last of the old Southampton - Channel Islands steamers, **Isle of Guernsey** which had been laid-up since the closure of that service on 12th May. Things returned to normal after a week at which time the last of the "Isles" was then sold for scrapping.

Thereafter, until 1975, the **Caesarea** and **Sarnia** partnership continued before they were both swallowed up by the changing trends in cross-Channel traffic. This is not to say that the sisters never departed from their normal Channel Islands services. During the first winter on the passage, Saturdays would see the **Caesarea** continue on to St. Malo then during December/January 1966/67 she moved to the Dover Strait to deputise for the **Invicta** on the fabled Dover (Admiralty Pier) - Calais "Golden Arrow" service just as the **Sarnia** had done in 1962/63. Visits to both ships almost thirty years ago, left one of the authors with the impression of light and mirrors in the **Sarnia** while the **Caesarea** was timbered, darker and far more traditional looking.

The 1963 season saw the end of the "three ship working" on the Weymouth - Channel Islands route with the lay-up of the **St. Patrick** on the completion of her summer season. After spending the 1964 season at Southampton, closing the St. Malo route, she moved to the Dover station at Christmas and remained there until her withdrawal in September 1971.

During celebrations in connection with the millennium of Mont St. Michel, the **Caesarea** was chartered for a round sailing from Weymouth to St. Malo in October 1966 while the **Sarnia** assisted on the Folkestone - Boulogne route the following Easter. There were occasions when Dover tonnage was required to help out at Weymouth and both the **St. Patrick** and **Maid of Orleans** were called to deputise when things were running less smoothly than they ought!

Although early in 1971, the **Caesarea** was sent for internal modifications which involved the resiting of her cafeteria and the creation of extra lounges, the arrival of the first car ferry on the Channel Islands route in 1973 saw the writing on the wall for the traditional service.

In her first season, the converted car ferry **Falaise** (the former Southampton - St. Malo passenger ship of 1947 and then displaced from the Newhaven - Dieppe link) ran only to Jersey as at that time Guernsey had not completed its linkspan.

Prior to her entry into service it had been the practise of carrying all Guernsey-bound vehicles in the mail boat's hold while sending cars for Jersey ahead in a cargo boat. Both vessels were timed to arrive at Jersey at about the same time and motorists could watch the cranes lift their valuable cars from the cargo vessel's hold onto the quayside. Sadly the old **Falaise**'s time on the new route was to be limited as during August 1975 she failed with terminal boiler problems. She was replaced by the chartered Swedish ferry **Svea Drott** which was eventually purchased by British Rail (Sealink) and renamed **Earl Godwin**. During the period of her conversion, several relief steamers helped out and the **Normannia** (since 1964, a Dover-based car ferry) and the former Stranraer vessel **Caledonian Princess**, both appeared prior the "new" ship coming on station in February 1976.

Before this time, it was obvious that the old order could not continue and on 6th October 1975, on her arrival from Jersey, the **Caesarea** moved up Weymouth harbour to lay-up pending her removal to commence a new career at Dover.

The fifteen year old steamer finally left the Dorset port on 3rd February 1976, entering the Wellington Dock at Dover later that day where she berthed adjacent to the Folkestone

car ferry **Hengist**. Her role at Dover was to take the place of the turbine passenger vessel, **Maid of Orleans** (1949) which, since the end of the **Invicta** in 1972 had operated the seasonal Dover - Calais service on approximately the old "Golden Arrow" timings.

After refit, the **Caesarea** sailed to Calais for dry-docking before entering service with Agents' Special sailings on the Folkestone - Boulogne route in time for Easter 1976. During her five year association with the Dover Strait services, she was required to operate between May and late September, after 1976 running two sailings a day and laying over at Calais at night. No Dover sailings were given in 1977 but her daily round otherwise ran Calais - Dover - Boulogne - Folkestone - Calais, or Calais - Folkestone - Boulogne - Dover - Calais. In April 1978, troubles with the new Channel Islands car ferry **Earl Godwin** (strike bound in dry-dock at Immingham) saw the **Caesarea** hastily recalled to Weymouth during which time the **Lord Warden** filled her roster.

At Weymouth, the **Normannia** and then the **Viking Victory** (from Townsend Thoresen) were also summoned, matters being complicated when the other car ferry, **Caledonian Princess**, had to go off for her own overhaul. With the **Normannia** unable to carry passengers, following an oil leak which made some of the stewards' cabins uninhabitable, the 17th April saw the small car ferry running with cars only while the **Caesarea** carried their passengers. On the conclusion of sailings on 6th May, both ships left the service for the final time.

The **Caesarea**'s last season started on 12th May, running a series of Agents' Specials to Ostend and ended on 27th September. Thereafter a series of "Farewell" day trips from Dover to Boulogne were organised until 4th October when on behalf of the Dover Rotary Club her Senior Master, Captain Mike Bodiam, chartered her to operate between Folkestone and Boulogne, the proceeds going to the RNLI.

It was then to Newhaven to lay-up but the steamer did not remain there for very long. She was in such good condition that she was soon sold to Apolina Ltd. of Hong Kong (trading as Superluck Enterprises), sailing from the Sussex port on 20th December as the **Aesarea**. Her delivery voyage took some five weeks and included calls at Gibraltar, Augusta (Sicily), Port Suez, Djibouti, Colombo, Singapore and Hong Kong. There she was painted all white with a pale yellow funnel and served as a hotel within the harbour although total conversion for hotel use does not appear to have happened.

A further reported sale to the Philippines occurred in 1984 when it was suggested that she was converted to diesel propulsion. Whatever the case, the **Aesarea** arrived at Kure, Japan, on 2nd April 1986, for further use as a floating hotel. Her new owners, Hiro Kisen K.K., abandoned their plans almost immediately and she sailed on 25th June for South Korean breakers.

*The **Aesarea** anchored in Hong Kong Harbour during 1981. Her role as a floating hotel was to end in failure.*   Photo: John Hendy collection.

M.V. **KEPPEL**

Built: 1961 Builder: Whites Shipyard (Southampton) Limited Speed: 9 knots
Dimensions: 110' x 27' Gross Tonnage: 214 tons.
Machinery: One Lister Blackstone 6 cylinder oil engine driving a single, Voith-Schneider propeller.
Owners/Operators: *British Transport Commission   1961 / 1963*
  British Railways Board   1963 / 1967
  Caledonian Steam Packet Co. Ltd. 1967 / 1973
  became Caledonian MacBrayne Limited 1973 to date

Many of the routes and services of Caledonian MacBrayne encompass some of Scotland's finest scenery and it could be said of the majority that they were as much a cruise as a routine voyage. In days and years gone by, numerous ships were employed on the River Clyde operating cruises and trips designed solely to enable people to get afloat and escape the industrial grime of Scotland's engineering cities. Gradually, the economics of the pleasure steamer business were rationalised and many that had survived earlier purges, finally fell victim to the Beeching Axe.

These days, just one such ship is operated by Caledonian MacBrayne and she is the small, but very attractive, *Keppel*.

Her story starts in 1961 in the unlikely setting of the River Thames where our ship, then named *Rose*, with her sisters *Catherine* and *Edith,* replaced veteran steam ferries of the same names on the Tilbury-Gravesend ferry for which British Railways, Eastern Region were responsible. There was also a vehicular ferry service which, using two ships, the *Tessa* (1924) and the *Mimie* (1927) lasted until 1964 when the commissioning of the Dartford Tunnel under the Thames rendered them redundant.

In addition to running the cross-river service, one vessel used to operate cruises to Greenwich and further upstream to Tower Pier. All three were virtually identical but could be separated at a distance by counting the number of black stripes on their one mast, which also doubled as an exhaust uptake as the ships had no funnels.

By late 1966, the Caledonian Steam Packet Company Limited, as it was then known, was in dire need of extra capacity to help replace their troublesome, diesel electric paddler, the *Talisman* which had previously been the mainstay of the Largs-Millport (Great Cumbrae) service.

British Railways, Eastern Region, let it be known that the *Rose* could be surplus to requirements and at the beginning of April 1967 ownership of the *Rose* duly passed "over the border" to Scotland.

The delivery voyage to the Clyde saw her boarded up and carrying fuel oil in drums lashed on deck. The trip took three weeks and the route taken was up the East Coast, to Inverness, through the famous Caledonian Canal and associated lochs to Fort William and then South, to the Clyde where the ship went into dock at Greenock for James Lamont & Co. Ltd. to do the necessary alterations.

The modifications included removal of the six hydraulic landing gangways which in their heyday had been capable of loading or discharging in a matter of minutes, her original complement. Without the luxury of floating stages to berth against, the Clyde's newest incumbent had to have a high level landing platform built on at wheelhouse level to facilitate the ship and her customers being able to come into contact with each other at low tide! She also had new toilet facilities built aft and a raised fo'c'sle to help her maintain the service in the often rougher waters of the Firth of Clyde.

After her alterations, the ship ran trials on the Skelmorlie measured mile and at almost 9 knots, she was considered adequate for her new role on the Largs-Millport route. Whilst she was amongst the slowest ships in the fleet, her Voith-Schneider propeller unit made her quite the most manoeuvrable and she duly took up service, still named **Rose**, on 12th June.

Shortly after, the **Rose** was re-christened **Keppel** (after an area of Cumbrae which she was destined to serve for almost twenty years) but for the time being, her port of registry remained as London.

Like the **Talisman** which she helped to replace, the **Keppel** was to be the lifeline for the Island of Cumbrae of which Millport is the principal township. Mail had to be collected, usually from Fairlie Pier and delivered to the Island. Schoolchildren and shoppers needed to travel conveniently to the "mainland" — indeed the ship was kept quite busy all the year round in the first few years of her new life.

After 1970 the A.B.C. class car ferry **Cowal** took over from the **Keppel** for the off season service which allowed the **Keppel** to lay-up and to be available for relief work and charters. She was really too small to be out in all winter weathers and carried no vehicles or cargo anyway. Two years later, a drive on-drive off service was started using new concrete slipways built at Largs and right opposite on Cumbrae, a few minutes sailing away. A redundant ferry from the Isle of Skye named **Coruish** started the new service

The **Rose** *arriving at Tilbury on 31st July 1965.   Photo: John Hendy.*

The **Keppel** *at "home" at Millport (Old Pier), Great Cumbrae, June 1985.   Photo: Richard Danielson.*

Passing Dumbarton Rock 21st May 1971. Photo: J. Aikman Smith

Sistership, the **Catherine** *in grey livery. Photo: John Hendy collection.*

Looking picturesque at Carrick Castle, 1986. Photo: Walter Bowie.

Passing Burns' "Highland Mary" at Dunoon. Photo: Walter Bowie.

The **Keppel** *and one of her successors, the* **Isle of Cumbrae**.

Photo: Richard Danielson.

and since then several ships, latterly new purpose-built ones, have served on the Cumbrae route.

Our ship, the **Keppel** was retained on the longer traditional route to Millport (Old Pier) in the peak summer months and her thirty minute crossing was one of the most pleasant short trips available. The waterfront at Millport is both picturesque and, some might say, a little quaint.

On occasions, the **Keppel** has had problems with her engine or Voith-Schneider propulsion unit and on 18th February 1980 on her evening return from Millport, she suffered a total power failure as a result of which she ended up on the rocks and most of her nine passengers were taken off by the Largs inshore lifeboat. An hour later with the aid of two fishing boats and CalMac's small ferry, the **Morvern**, she was towed back to the safety of Largs and then she sailed to Troon for permanent repairs.

The state of Millport (Old Pier) and the economics of operating the **Keppel**'s traditional long route (compared with the short one to the new Cumbrae slipway) sounded the beginning of discussion which in the end was to bring about the closure of the route.

Local opinion favoured retaining the **Keppel** and there was even talk of the Islanders buying her to run their own service. CalMac and the various authorities and councils deliberated. On 14th December 1984, Strathclyde Regional Council published the following notice. "Millport Town Pier - Due to storm damage, the Millport Town Pier is closed to the public until further notice."

In the event, the Pier was patched-up and the **Keppel** sailed again as summer boat in 1985 whilst all the necessary authorities went through the formalities of administering the last rites to enable them to bring about the closure of the route. The reader might be forgiven for thinking that the matter had become unduly protracted as the **Keppel** emerged again in 1986 for what was definitely to be the last season's

operation of the Largs to Millport (Old Pier) route. In fact, she ran from mid May to the end of June after which, on 1st July, the two new ferries finally took up the roll on-roll off service to Cumbrae Slip on the Island's north east corner.

The **Keppel** then took on her present role as successor to the long line of distinguished Caledonian Company cruising vessels — ships that made voyages solely for their passengers' pleasure.

Since 1986, the **Keppel** has sailed a most interesting pattern of cruises linking harbours and piers that were in danger of becoming the merest, faint memories, somewhere in the back of peoples' minds. 1988, the year of the Glasgow Garden Festival, saw her running weekend cruises upriver to Renfrew and the Garden Festival site too.

The storms of winter 1989/90 caused widespread carnage. Millport (Old Pier) was severely damaged yet again and it was thought likely that it might never be fit for further use. The storms wreaked havoc with Helensburgh Pier too and whilst the **Keppel**, with her small size, was able to carry on using the Pier in the summer of 1990, its regular customer, the legendary paddler steamer **Waverley** was unable to do so. This gave the opportunity for the **Keppel** (in addition to her normal cruising schedules) to be chartered to the **Waverley** organisation on July and August Saturdays with the little ship, providing a welcome feeder service to the much larger paddle steamer which awaited her passengers at Gourock.

1990 found the ship looking and running better than ever in recent memory and she is a credit to all who are involved with her operation.

During the whole of 1991, Millport (Old Pier) will be completely closed to shipping as, thankfully, it is to be rebuilt. Hopefully, when it reopens in 1992, the **Keppel**, our erstwhile Tilbury-Gravesend ferry, will be there in pride of place, just as she was on 12th June 1967 when she started her new life, "north of the border".

T.S.S. **KING GEORGE V**

Built: 1926	Builders: Wm. Denny & Bros., Dumbarton
Speed: 20 knots	Dimensions: 260' x 32'
Gross Tonnage: 791 to 985 tons at various times	
	Machinery: See text - Parsons geared turbines, twin screw, 3,500 shp
Owner/Operator:	Turbine Steamers Ltd 1926/1935
	David MacBrayne Ltd. 1935/1973
	became Caledonian MacBrayne Ltd. 1973/1975
	C. H. Bailey Group 1975/1980

For over 30 years, the turbine steamer **King George V** graced the popular West Highland resort of Oban. The fact that such a small town was able to support a vessel of her size not only says much for the grandeur and beauty of the coastal scenery but also for her two most popular calling places — the islands of Staffa and Iona. The former with its basalt columns, formidable cliffs and the deep and dramatic Fingal's cave, which was immortalised by Mendelssohn during his visit there in 1829, and the latter which represents the birthplace of Scottish Christianity following St. Columba's arrival from Ireland in the 6th century.

The **King George V** however was not built for the Oban excursion traffic, with which her proud name will always be associated, but for the longer Firth of Clyde sailings of Turbine Steamers Ltd.. Her frames were set on 29th December 1925 after which building followed quickly and she was launched on 29th April 1926. Trials however did not take place until 7th September when the ship clocked 20.78 knots between the Cloch and Cumbrae.

Although she was built on the same lines as the previous Clyde turbine excursion steamers, the "KG V" was the first such vessel to have a large part of her promenade deck totally enclosed giving passengers outstanding views and welcome cover when the weather proved inclement. When new, the ship was fitted with experimental high pressure machinery which was built and fitted by Parsons, the inventors of the steam turbine, at a cost of £29,000. Four quadruple expansion ahead turbines were fitted to the port side while the starboard set comprised triple expansion only. The then white funnelled steamer was a coal burner and was provided with bunker space for up to 43 tons. Although her contract price was £68,500 her final cost was £69,648 and as will have been seen by the date of her official trials, she missed all but the tail-end of the 1926 excursion season.

In 1927, the **King George V** was placed upon the long day cruise to Campbeltown, on the Kintyre peninsula, or on the more sheltered haul up lengthy Loch Fyne to Inverary, replacing the premier turbine steamer **King Edward** on these rosters.

Two years later, Babcock & Wilcox boilers replaced the original unreliable boilers and in 1932 her accommodation was modified. More changes were to take place in 1935 when the steamer and her owners were taken over by David MacBrayne Ltd. (since 1928 themselves a jointly owned subsidiary of the London Midland & Scottish Railway and Coast Lines Ltd.). Both the **King George V** and her partner

This classic scene shows the one and only **King George V** at anchor in the Sound of Iona during a Round Mull cruise in June 1973. *Photo: John Hendy.*

Polished brass and gleaming varnish!   *Photo: John Hendy.*

Resting at Oban's Railway Pier after a Round Mull cruise in June 1973. Photo: John Hendy.

The **King George V** *arrives at Oban for the Coastal Cruising Association Round Jura charter on 3rd September 1972.   Photo: Andrew Jones.*

Queen Alexandra now adopted the familiar scarlet funnels, the latter ship gaining a rare, third funnel in the process, when she reappeared as the *Saint Columba*.

MacBrayne's "new" ships were the first turbine ships they ever owned and replaced the much-loved but quite antique paddle steamers *Iona* (1864) and *Columba* (1878) which were retired after the 1935 season.

Before taking up service for her new owners, the *King George V* was sent back to Denny's Leven shipyard for further modifications to her engines. She was reboiled again, receiving a single double ended Scotch boiler with 200lb. per square inch working pressure (this against the 575 p.s.i. of the original twin high pressure superheated water tube boilers). The refit also saw the simplification of her turbine arrangement, as the additional port h.p. turbine was removed. New funnels, of greater diameter, were fitted and in 1936 she took over the Oban - Iona service from the five year old diesel-electric vessel *Lochfyne* which was switched to the Fort William route. The turbine steamer soon made her mark and became the most popular excursion vessel of her generation, operating as she did, on the most magnificent of all coastal cruises.

The outbreak of war in 1939 saw the *King George V* acting as a tender on the Clyde until at the end of May 1940, she sailed south to Dover making six trips to Dunkirk assisting with the evacuation of the British Expeditionary Force. After this most gallant service, she returned to the Clyde again acting as a tender to the troopships arriving at the Tail of the Bank with Commonwealth and American troops on board.

In April 1946, the *King George V*'s first post-war season saw her as the Ardrishaig mail steamer operating from Gourock, a service on which she was to reappear from time to time. It was back to Oban in 1947 where she was to both reign and remain until the end of the 1974 season giving

In the Sound of Iona again as excursionists come ashore to visit the Sacred Isle. Photo: A. A. MacGregor.

*Sheer Majesty! The **King George V** is seen, with the sun behind her, in the Kyles of Bute during September 1952.* Photo: J. M. Guy.

remarkable service and gaining a following second only to the paddle steamer **Columba** herself.

The year 1950 saw the steamer converted to burn fuel oil which resulted in the 24 year old ship running faster than ever. Minor changes in her appearance help make photographic identification a little easier: in 1952 she received a mainmast, radar was installed in 1958 while in the following year, inflatable liferafts were fitted and her six lifeboats were reduced to four, just as she was up to 1936.

In 1962, the beautiful restaurant was extended and other minor modifications over a period of several overhauls raised her gross tonnage to 985. There was nothing better, on her circuits of Mull, when, shortly after leaving Iona, one descended the companionway to her Dining Saloon for High Tea and watched the Ross of Mull slip by out of the port windows - sheer enjoyment! Cruises to Iona from Fort William, some of them south-about and some weekend ferry work from Oban up the Sound of Mull to Tobermory were also included in her itinerary as were excursions into Loch Sunart and south to the Isles of the Sea.

The Coastal Cruising Association took the **King George V** on an anti-clockwise circumnavigation of the island of Jura in September 1972, the first time the sailing had been given since the **Queen Alexandra** (1902) had done it seventy years previously. In the following year the CCA attempted to take her around Rhum but sadly strong winds prevented her from leaving the shelter of the Sound of Mull. Instead, a Loch Sunart cruise and a circuit of Lismore Island were substituted.

Caledonian MacBrayne was formed on 1st January 1973 when David MacBrayne Ltd. and the Caledonian Steam Packet Co. Limited merged to form a single fleet. The familiar red funnels were adorned with a yellow disk upon which the lion rampant of Scotland was placed. The "KG V's" lions actually came from the Clyde-based turbine steamer **Duchess of Hamilton** which was withdrawn from service at the end of the previous season.

With the steamer by then in the twilight of her days, annual overhauls and surveys became increasingly expensive. This coupled with the Arab-Israeli War, which pushed up oil prices to a then astronomical extent, an event which affected all fares, was to have a drastic effect on passenger carryings. Although it was hoped that the **King George V** would see her half century, sadly this was not to be and on 15th September 1974, the steamer ended what was to be her final season and later sailed to Greenock for winter lay-up. Although there were rumours concerning her possible withdrawal, it was not until 19th December that Caledonian MacBrayne's General Manager broke the sad news, "with extreme reluctance". Immediately meetings were held in Oban to gather support to buy the ship on behalf of the local tourist association and she even underwent mechanical overhaul before, early in 1975, she was placed in the hands of shipbrokers. An offer of £32,000 was apparently made by a German group who had designs on running her on Rhine cruises. This was countered by a rival bid from some Glasgow businessmen but nothing final was forthcoming by the date of the deadline for offers on 18th March. On 2nd April a sale was announced and on 19th April she left Scottish shores for the last time, being towed by the tug **Mumbles** to Cardiff where she had been purchased by Nationwide Transport, a member of the C.H. Bailey Group, for possible conversion to a restaurant.

Sadly, little appears to have happened to the veteran turbine steamer which was marooned in the Mountstuart Drydock. Just when it appeared that she had no future at all, unexpectedly Bass Charrington took an interest in her to replace their Thames-based floating pub and restaurant **Old Caledonia,** which had been gutted by fire at her berth adjacent to Waterloo Bridge in April 1980. Suddenly, after years of neglect, work began on board the **King George V.**

Laid-up at East India Harbour, Greenock in 1974. Photo: Walter Bowie.

The King is dead — Long live the King! Cardiff 1981. Photo: John Hendy collection.

Ardnamurchan to starboard.   Photo: *John Hendy.*

Coll ahead.   Photo: *John Hendy.*

Looking astern at Scarba.   Photo: *John Hendy.*

Fingal's Cave — Island of Staffa.   Photo: *John Hendy.*

Whether or not she would have gained the necessary Load Line Exemption and other certificates necessary for the long tow to London is not known. The matter sadly became academic when, on the night of 25th-26th August 1981, she too was gutted by fire. August 1981 was a bad month for British excursion steamers claiming not only the graceful **King George V** but also the ***Prince Ivanhoe*** (ex. ***Shanklin***) which was lost off the Gower peninsula.

So ended the career of possibly the most splendid and magnificent of all British turbine excursion steamers. Everything about her seemed perfect. Her flare, her sheer, the rake of her lofty masts and black topped red funnels, the glistening paintwork, the shining varnish and the dazzling brass! Above all, there was the vibration free hum of her boiler fans and turbines which allowed her passengers to be "at one" with the ship and their surroundings. It was a perfect place from which to enjoy the unique sights and sounds of the islands of Mull, Staffa and the romantic solitude of Iona itself. Many would say that the **King George V** was simply unsurpassed.

The incomparable **King George V** *slips into Oban on a late summer's day in the 1950's.*   Photo: J. M. Guy.

T.S.M.V. **LORD OF THE ISLES**

Built: 1989
Speed: 16 knots
Gross Tonnage: 3,504 tons
Machinery: 2 x Mirlees Blackstone diesels, total 5,792 bhp
Owner/Operator: Caledonian MacBrayne Limited 1989 to date

Builder: Appledore Ferguson, Port Glasgow
Dimensions: 275' x 52'

For well over a century, the ships of Caledonian MacBrayne Limited and its various individual predecessors whose principal names the Company now bears, have served Scotland's River Clyde and its Western Highlands and Islands with a reliability and frequency sufficient to enable local life to develop, prosper and flourish. The history of the **Lord of the Isles** owes it origins to an era long before the advent of today's roll on - roll off ferries and a brief look into the past here, is not inappropriate. In those much earlier times, when travel and communications between Scotland's remoter islands was by sail or early steamer, the islanders' mobility and contact with the outside world was sparse. Their indigenous populations, especially the poorer people, whose working lives then centred on agriculture, fishing and other traditional or "cottage" industries would spend long periods of near isolation in their own communities, many never venturing off their native island soil. Only then were elementary piers and harbours being constructed.

Later, in the late 1800s, the railways reached the coast and with them, came the proliferation of existing steamer services, many of which were the direct ancestors of today's modern ferry network. Over the years, along with the greater distribution of wealth, travel has gradually become within the reach of most people, including those who, for what ever reason, could not resist the call to leave the islands. More so today, there are also those from the "mainland" who, if only for a week or two each year, hanker for the quiet, relatively uncommercial, crime-free Hebridean life.

In addition to passengers, the ships began to be filled with the world's wider choice of goods and "necessities", not forgetting the product of the all-pervading mail order catalogue in the 1960s. Neither was the business all one way, with exports of famous tweeds, liquor and other unique Hebridean produce helping to swell the islands' economies.

Loading ships by crane and derrick became a thing of the past and cargo started to move on wheels, becoming completely mobile through containerisation and by being put on pallets capable of mechanical movement and stowage. Gone were the days of the horse and cart and the porter's barrow! Inevitably the design of the ships, with large vehicle decks and comfortable all weather passenger accommodation, was adapted to meet the new demands and in the **Lord of the Isles**, we see the ultimate in this type of ferry design.

Transport and tourism have now become a driving force in the islands and of their economies. Whilst cheap air transport was responsible for the demise of the world's great passenger liners, the vast number of services needed to connect the remote island communities has, to a large extent, enabled that myriad of sea- borne lifelines to survive, rationalised, but otherwise unfettered.

On 7th March 1989, Mrs Malcolm Rifkind, wife of the then Secretary of State for Scotland, launched the multipurpose

*The **Lord of the Isles** meets her element for the first time on launch day, 7th March 1989.*   Photo: George Young, Photographers.

MAX HEADROOM 16 FEET

The **Lord of the Isles,** *well laden with prefabricated houses for shipment to the Outer Isles.*

Photo: Walter Bowie.

passenger and vehicle ferry **Lord of the Isles**, and in so doing, christened the fourth vessel in Caledonian MacBrayne's present fleet to exceed 3,000 gross tons.

When launched, the ship was in an advanced state of completion and remaining fitting-out proceeded quickly in the James Watt Dock at Greenock. It was then in to the Garvel Dry-dock to enable the shipyard launching shackles and other impedimenta to be removed following which, the **Lord of the Isles** was ready to run trials at the end of April. After acceptance, she was handed over to CalMac on 19th May, then visited Coll and Tiree on 20th, and the Outer Isles on 21st. She took up service the next day, 22nd May 1989.

The **Lord of the Isles** is based at Oban and normally is to be found operating the routes to the inner isles of Coll and Tiree (sometimes calling at Tobermory, Mull en route) and on the outer Hebrides service to Lochboisdale and Castlebay on South Uist and Barra. Her entry into service enabled both the **Columba** and the **Claymore** to be displaced. Britain's membership of Europe facilitated a grant from the European Regional Development Fund to be forthcoming in respect of the building of the ship, the total cost of which exceeded £6.93 million.

Steeped in history, sometimes older than time itself, the Western Isles provide a wealth of different interests for the visiting tourist. From the most active sports and pastimes to the purely passive, all combine to attract today's visitor. From far afield and every walk of life they come in search of the past and the present, both real and legendary, cultural and physical. The Islands can satisfy every taste. The **Lord of the Isles**, "LOTI" as she has been nicknamed, has proved to be the latest instrument by which the wider development of the Hebridean Islands has been achieved for the good of everyone.

Today, passengers, cars, caravans, coaches and lorries are carried in numbers that would have been beyond comprehension not so long ago, with over six million passengers and one and a quarter million cars being carried by Caledonian MacBrayne on all their routes, every year.

Whilst the outer Hebridean destinations have linkspans, the inner islands of Coll and Tiree (the latter holding unlikely combined records as one of Britain's sunniest and windiest places) do not, and with their exposed positions, the vessel operating that service is best equipped with a very speedy hoist so that when the ship is ranging about on the pier face in the swell, no harm is done. It is hoped that it will not be too long before linkspan installations will be provided at these two islands. However, ownership of the piers and funding are both major problems requiring Caledonian MacBrayne, Regional and Central Governmental decisions which all take time and lots of money.

As a result of the building of the **Lord of the Isles**, the faithful old **Glen Sannox** (1957), the hoist of which was anything but quick, was able to be withdrawn and was sold for service in the Mediterranean Sea in August 1989, renamed **Knooz**.

Operating all the year round, the **Lord of the Isles** holds a Class IIA passenger certificate for 506, has all the latest lifesaving equipment as part of her extensive specification and can also carry 67 cars or 9 large commercial vehicles. On her overnight sailings, 18 two berth, private cabins are available for passengers, highlighting the fact that the modern ship is designed for "round the clock" working. She is fully stabilised too, a comfort factor nowadays found on all Caledonian MacBrayne's large ships.

On the principle that ships do not earn any money whilst they are tied-up in harbour, in recent years Caledonian MacBrayne have been wanting to schedule their Western Isles' fleet to operate seven days a week. There has been opposition to this by those observers of the Sabbath who feel that a Sunday service to the islands is neither desirable nor justified and the matter continues to be debated noisily and publicly. Hopefully, the commercial realities will reveal themselves to the scheme's opponents and the obvious necessity to have the multi-million pound ferry fleet at work all the time, will prevail.

On 12th March 1990, at the end of her first year in operation, which included plenty of wild, winter weather at the beginning of 1990, the **Lord of the Isles** went back to Greenock for survey and dry-docking, where she remained until April 2nd before re-entering service.

The **Lord of the Isles** is a powerful, solid ship but, on the rare occasions that the hostile Atlantic Ocean has impinged and really bad weather interceded, it has proved convenient for her to swap schedules with the larger, **Isle of Mull** which normally sails to Craignure (Mull).

Livestock movements (vital to the island farming communities) unusual cargoes on offer and survey and overhaul reliefs have also caused ships to exchange otherwise regular duties.

Now just two years old, the **Lord of the Isles** has already proved herself to the Hebridean Islands that she serves and has given them the best regular service they have ever enjoyed. She is a worthy successor to a long line of fine ships that have flown the Caledonian and MacBrayne banners.

Caledonian MacBrayne
Hebridean and Clyde Ferries

(Right) *The* **Lord of the Isles** *at Garvel Dry-dock, Greenock on 29th March 1990.* *Photo: L. McDuff*

The **Lord Warden** *steams away from Dover's Eastern Docks on passage to Boulogne during the 1973 season. Notice that her starboard belting has received something of a battering and that the single lorry on her vehicle deck proves that she could carry* some *freight!*
Photo: John Hendy collection.

(Right) The view from Dover's No. 2 linkspan of the **Lord Warden's** *car deck in August 1966.* *Photo: John Hendy.*

(Above) The **Lord Warden** coming into Boulogne in 1969 with stern gates open for swift vehicle disembarkation. Such practices would be forbidden today.   Photos: Andrew Jones.

(Right) A most unusual view of the **Lord Warden** on overhaul immediately after receiving the new British Rail livery in October 1964.. The black paint on her 'fireman's helmet' funnel extension was later, thankfully, lowered.   Photo: John Hendy collection.

T.S.S. **LORD WARDEN**

Built: 1952 Builder: William Denny & Bros., Dumbarton. Speed: 20 knots Dimensions: 362' x 60' Gross Tonnage: 3,333 tons Machinery: Twin screw, double reduction geared turbines 8,000 shp. Two Babcock & Wilcox water tube boilers, closed stokehold forced draught.

Owners/Operators: British Transport Commission 1952/1963
British Railways Board 1963/1969
British Rail (Shipping & International Services Division) 1969/1979

Sealink U.K. Ltd. 1979
Ahmed Mohamed Baaboud Trading & Shipping Agency, Saudi Arabia 1979/1981

During the 28 years in which the turbine steam ship **Lord Warden** was on service, she was to see a complete re-emphasis in the role of vessels of her type. The roll on - roll off revolution of the late sixties was to see the "Warden" transformed from the model car ferry operating a cosy, seasonal holiday/tourist trade to an obsolete secondary vessel, outmoded due to her inability to carry the all important freight traffic.

The **Lord Warden** was England's first, specially constructed drive on - drive off cross-Channel car ferry and in her building displayed the typical lines of a Denny, Dumbarton, ship. In those days, the lines of the new vehicle carriers had far more in common with the classic passenger steamers than they did with the modern ro-ro types we see today.

The history of the early days of the car ferry on the Dover Strait is well documented in our book "The Townsend Thoresen Years" but the **Lord Warden** was to join the one time Southampton—St. Malo steamer **Dinard** *(see page 62)* which had operated a lift on - lift off service from Dover (Admiralty Pier) to Boulogne (Bassin Loubet) since July 1947.

With the new Yard No. 1455 building at Dumbarton, the Boulogne Chamber of Commerce undertook the construction of a linkspan at berth 13 and Dover Harbour Board drew up plans for a pair of linkspans in their Eastern Docks, at what was then the quiet end of the harbour.

The "Warden" was duly launched into the River Leven by Mrs. John Elliot on 14th December 1951. On trials she reached 21.22 knots, she sailed south on 28th April 1952 and was delivered to the Southern Region of British Railways at Southampton two days later.

Delays with the Boulogne linkspan saw a postponement in the "Warden's" entry into service and it was not until 14th July that she arrived at Dover to undertake a special VIP/ press voyage two days later. On 17th July she entered service — the first car ferry to carry more than 100 cars.

Her Master was Captain G.D. (Tony) Walker DSC, who had transferred from the former "Golden Arrow" steamer **Canterbury** to see the Southern Region's prestige steamer into service. Sadly it was not to be a happy debut for the ship as on 23th July, serious turbine troubles sent her back to Southampton. The **Dinard** was quickly transferred into her schedules and out of the Wellington Dock at Dover came the train ferry **Hampton Ferry** to take the secondary roster. Both she and her sister **Shepperton Ferry** had been adapted to carry 65 cars in their wing roads during the winter of 1950 in order to help out during the busy summer months. With the "Warden's" damaged turbine having to be sent back to Dumbarton for repairs, the new ship was off service for a whole month and missed the lucrative holiday season.

In January 1953, the **Lord Warden** carried her first car deck full of Monte Carlo Rally entrants, putting the 107 vehicles ashore at Boulogne in 20 minutes. At the end of that month, severe storms saw Stranraer's car ferry **Princess Victoria** lost on passage to Larne, the seas smashing through her stern gates and flooding the car deck, eventually bringing about a capsize. The "Warden" was fitted with similar gates — they were not doors — one could stand inside them on the vehicle deck and look astern.

Eight days after this tragedy, heavy seas off Boulogne stove in the **Lord Warden**'s gates during a routine passage to Dover. Very little water was taken in and they were quickly shored-up. The stays were immediately strengthened and the vessel was not even taken out of service. However, following the publication of the report into the loss of the **Princess Victoria**, large scuppers were cut into the car deck to allow any water to drain away quickly.

In April 1953, the **Lord Warden** was in Southampton having her fin stabilisers fitted, those originally intended for her being sent to John Brown's yard at Clydebank for installation in the Royal Yacht **Britannia**. On 15th June 1953, the "Warden" was present at the Coronation Review in Spithead. With Dover's £750,000 car ferry terminal officially open at the end of the same month, the ship could now be operated as her designers intended.

The following winter saw the Dover and Folkestone "Railway" steamers all fitted with radiophones thereby allowing direct voice communication between ship and shore. Then on 26th

*On trials in the Clyde, the **Lord Warden** makes a fine sight.*

Photo: Glasgow University Archives.

May 1954, the "Warden" made history by giving the first television broadcast from a moving ship at sea. On one of the roughest days of the year, the inimitable Richard Dimbleby set about interviewing Capt. Walker on the bridge wing when, to quote Dimbleby's own words, a wave "the size of a mountain" crashed over the "Warden's" bows, drenching all those present and sending the cameraman plus vital equipment flying across the ship's teak decks. The broadcast however, went on!

To show the easy life that the ship enjoyed in those early days, the "Kentish Express" reported in January 1956 that she was just off for a "spring clean" taking 200 men seven weeks at a cost of £10,000. The ship's most unhappy time was undoubtedly on 7th July 1956 when she was in collision in thick fog off Cap Gris Nez with the French motor vessel **Tamba**. The "Warden" received serious bow damage and was off service for five weeks at Southampton. The **Shepperton Ferry** replaced her on the car ferry link and in order to assist, Townsend's **Halladale** also put on extra sailings.

Capt. Walker retired in October 1958 and the "Warden's" senior Master became Captain Walter Coulter. The same month saw the old **Dinard** depart while during the following May, the new **Maid of Kent** entered service. From then until 1970, both she and the **Lord Warden** maintained the Dover - Boulogne car ferry link being assisted from 1964 by the converted **Normannia** and in the following year by the new **Dover**. February 1969 (and again in February 1972) briefly saw the "Warden" on the passenger only "Golden Arrow" link between Dover (Admiralty Pier) and Calais.

Problems with funnel emissions being sucked into the accommodation by a badly placed air intake system immediately astern of the funnel were countered in 1957 when two quite hideous stovepipes appeared, to disperse the offending fumes. Similar problems also existed in the passenger steamer **Maid of Orleans** (3,777 gross tons, built 1949) and

The **Lord Warden** seen leaving Folkestone on a Boulogne passenger sailing in June 1972. Photo: Andrew Jones.

The **Lord Warden** and SNCF's new **Chantilly** at Dover's Eastern Docks on 26th August 1966. Photo: John Hendy.

*The **Lord Warden** being towed to the fitting-out basin shortly after her launch at Dumbarton on 14th December 1951. Denny's own tug/tender* **The Second Snark** *is to be seen on the left of the photograph (see also page 60 in Book I of this series). Today she is still in service as a pleasure "steamer" on the Clyde.* Photo: Glasgow University Archives.

in April 1959 she had been given a funnel extension with a "fireman's helmet" in order to help matters. The "Warden" duly received a similar "cap" during the following winter when the stove pipes were thankfully removed.

The old order of British Rail car ferries sailing to Boulogne and SNCF vessels to Calais was ended in 1970 when the **Lord Warden** was switched to the Calais link to operate with the French motor vessels **Compiègne** and **Chantilly**. In the spring of 1971 she worked the Holyhead - Dun Laoghaire service for the first time and in the following year was again booked to work the crossing. Unfortunately, the unrest saw a falling off in bookings and she was laid-up all season at Newhaven.

Seasonal use with the odd winter outing returned as, for example in January 1976, when the steamer was hastily brought out of mothballs to run the overnight Folkestone - Ostend service. In the summer of 1977 both the **Lord Warden** and the **Normannia** were required to work just three daily round trips between Dover and Boulogne. Easter 1978 saw the "Warden" appear on the Weymouth - Cherbourg link in place of her one time running partner **Maid of Kent** which had been delayed on overhaul.

For the summer of 1978, the ship was switched to the Fishguard station where she was required to operate a new 5 hour 30 minute crossing of the Irish Sea to Dun Laoghaire and a new night crossing on the traditional route to Rosslare. For this service, her original stern gates were replaced with a much higher set of doors up to poop deck level. An athwartship girder across the top of the stern entrance was also fitted thereby prohibiting the carriage of any high-sided vehicles. Prior to this, the steamer had always been able to carry at least one lorry! That November, the **Lord Warden** was summoned back to the Dover Strait for the final time to stand in for the French ferry **Compiègne** on the Boulogne - Dover passage. A daily crossing during the three week spell

of service revived many happy memories for her devotees.

The year 1979 saw the "Warden's" final spell of U.K. service. After a period on the Fishguard - Rosslare link during March, she was laid-up in the dock at Milford Haven before emerging to supplement the St. George's Channel sailings of Sealink's new monster, **Stena Normandica**. When the latter vessel developed serious engine troubles, the "Warden" came to the rescue before she exchanged routes with the larger **Avalon** and sailed north to Holyhead where, as from 12th July, she accompanied the **St. Columba**. At the end of the season she came to the rescue again when the "Columba" failed and the Dun Laoghaire service was left in the capable hands of Denny ship number 1455 for six days. Her final crossing ended on 8th September when she tied up in the Welsh port at 19.15 under the command of Capt. Bakewell. Two days later she sailed again for lay-up at Newhaven. In late October came the news that the **Lord Warden** had been sold to the Baaboud Trading and Shipping Agency of Jeddah. She was towed to Southampton on 15th November and bade farewell to the British shores on 2nd January 1980 when she sailed out through the Solent as the **Al Zaher**.

The Saudis used the 28 year old steamer mainly as a livestock carrier across the Red Sea but this sad state of affairs did not last long. On 25th April 1981 she arrived for breaking by Karum Shipbreaking Industries at Gadani Beach, Pakistan.

So ended the notable career of a pioneer ship. The constant comings and goings of today's modern short-sea fleets are ample testimony to the **Lord Warden's** early success. Whether or not today's units will serve their owners for as long and as faithfully as she did and whether or not they will engender the same spirit of happiness and loyalty amongst their crews remains to be seen. Of one fact we may be certain: there will never be another **Lord Warden**!

Coming astern across Dover Harbour in 1952.
Photo: John Hendy collection.

The "Warden" leaves Holyhead on 9th August 1979.
Photo: Dick Richards.

Laid-up in Dover's Wellington Dock in October 1974.
Photo: John Hendy.

The **Al Zaher** (ex **Lord Warden**) at Jeddah in February 1981.
Photo: Ambrose Greenway.

The **Mona's Isle** *approaching Llandudno on Sunday, 20th August 1978.*

Photo: John Shepherd.

T.S.S. **MONA'S ISLE** (V)

Built: 1951 Builder: Cammell Laird, Birkenhead.
Speed: 21 knots Dimensions 344' x 47' Gross Tonnage: 2,491 tons
Machinery: Twin screw, single reduction geared Parsons turbines, constructed by Cammell Laird. High and low pressure turbines geared to each shaft. 8,500 shp. Three Babcock & Wilcox water tube, oil fired boilers, closed stokehold, forced draught.
Owner/Operator: The Isle of Man Steam Packet Company Limited

The **Mona's Isle** was launched on 12th October 1950 by Mrs E. A. Kitto, wife of one of the Manx directors of the Steam Packet Company, at the famous Merseyside shipyard of Cammell Laird & Co Limited (Shipbuilders and Engineers). She was the fifth in a series of virtually identical passenger ships commissioned by the Isle of Man Steam Packet Company as replacements for their depleted and war damaged fleet, the total investment costing in excess of £2,500,000.

The other four, named in order of arrival on service, were the **King Orry** and **Mona's Queen** (1946) **Tynwald** (1947) and **Snaefell** (1948).

At the launching ceremony, Company Chairman Mr J. F. Crellin praised Cammell Laird and the ship designers thus: "It is an extraordinarily fine thing for the designers of the **King Orry** that they could repeat the ship four times, with only minor alterations. The previous four ships have done exceptionally fine work and we have had no trouble with any of them". He went on to note that Fleet Commodore, Captain J. W. Cubbon preferred to keep his Commodore's flag flying in the **Ben-my-Chree** (1927) rather than take over the new ship. Also, not only had Mrs Kitto launched the vessel, but earlier she had actually chosen the upholstery and soft furnishings for the ship.

The launch made the main front page story in the "Isle of Man Examiner" dated 13th October 1950, which covered the event in great detail, and featured two fine photographs of the ship and her sponsor, Mrs Kitto. The piece was almost poetic and commenced like this:

"Lying snugly this morning under the grim, towering hull of the gigantic aircraft carrier, **Ark Royal**, at Cammell Laird's shipyard at Birkenhead is the new, spick and span **Mona's Isle**, launched yesterday in a blaze of autumn sunshine".

After fitting out, the well proportioned **Mona's Isle** left her builders' basin on 15th March 1951 on the tide at 02.30 and proceeded to anchor midstream in the river. At the more reasonable hour of 08.30, officials and dignitaries were ferried out to the ship from the Birkenhead Ferries' Woodside stage, and then set sail for the Bar Lightship, marking the entrance to the Mersey Estuary. En route, compasses would have been adjusted and checked, Direction Finding equipment (D.F.) calibrated and the ship worked up to full power. The records show that the Mersey Pilot was disembarked prior to tests beginning. Thereafter, the steering gear was tried out with the ship travelling at full speed, turning tests were carried out with the helm both to starboard and then to port with timings taken for each and finally, the emergency steering, operated from the wheel right aft, was given the

Launch day, 12th October 1950. The **Mona's Isle** *awaits her sponsor, Mrs. E. A. Kitto and on the launch platform (extreme right) the photographer prepares his camera for the moment that the champagne cascades over the bow of the ship. Down in Cammell Laird's adjacent dry-dock on the left, the Company's cargo boat* **Peveril** *is suitably dressed overall for the great event.* Photo: Capt. Westby Kissack collection.

standard, very tough test. After all, it had to be capable of steering the ship to safety in the unlikely event of all else having failed!

The ship was then brought to a standstill and the astern turbines were given steam for astern running and bow rudder tests using the port and starboard helm wheels separately, up on the flying bridge. The vessel then proceeded to Douglas where she was due to call for about an hour prior to sailing north, overnight, to the Clyde, for her official trials on the world-famous, Skelmorlie mile the next day.

Captain Albert Whiteway brought the **Mona's Isle** to Douglas for the first time later that day and she berthed, briefly, at the north side of the King Edward Pier to collect the Island trials' party. These thirteen local people included His Excellency the Lieutenant Governor, His Honour Deemster (Manx High Court Judge) Cowley and three Manx Directors of the Steam Packet Company.

Next morning, Friday 16th March, in moderate sea conditions, the ship was put through her paces and made the usual, three double runs of the Skelmorlie measured mile. Starting at 09.30 the six miles were carefully logged with the ship working up to her full 9,750 shp for the last two, one in each direction. 21.87 knots was recorded for the final run with propellers turning at 287 r.p.m.

With all the tests satisfactorily completed, the **Mona's Isle** left the Clyde, bound for the Island in order to disembark the trials' party. Unfortunately, a severe gale blew up on the way and it was deemed unwise to attempt to berth at any of the Island's harbours with the new and virtually untried ship. The ship proceeded on to the Mersey, only to find it was fog bound! As radar was not fitted to the ship until 1955, there was no alternative but for the **Mona's Isle** to anchor at the Mersey Bar and await clearer visibility.

Next morning, her older sistership, the **Mona's Queen**, on the service route from Liverpool to Douglas had left the Landing Stage at 11.28, a little later than usual on account of the fog and was groping her way downstream still in poor visibility. Detailed research of all the available records shows that at 13.18, the **Mona's Queen** hove-to in the vicinity of the Bar Lightship for nine minutes, in order to embark the trials' party from the **Mona's Isle**. In a trip described as "unusual and not unexciting", the intrepid dignitaries were transferred to the Douglas bound **Mona's Queen** using the **Mona's Isle's** motor lifeboat!

The specification books for all the ships of the class demanded very high standards and whilst no money was to be spent unnecessarily, quality was the prime consideration. "All timber for spars, decks, cabins whatsoever, to be of the very best quality throughout." "The workmanship throughout the vessel is to be of the very best and highest character." These two short extracts were typical of the owners' instructions to the builders. In the event, no one was disappointed and Cammell Laird produced a fine ship that served the Island well for thirty years.

In her long and interesting career, the **Mona's Isle** was, like most of the Company's passenger vessels, mainly employed in the frantic summer operations beginning with the world famous motorcycle T.T. races traffic in June each year and then building up with busy weekend holiday and high season tourist traffic. In the winter, just two passenger ships were in service and the others were laid-up in Birkenhead and Barrow. The **Mona's Isle** was not normally a winter boat but it was not unheard of for her to emerge out of season to take her share of relief sailings.

In the early spring, the vessels would emerge, one by one, from lay-up for dry-docking, repainting and annual survey for passenger certificate. The shipyards would have liked the work to be spread more evenly throughout the autumn and winter months when their labour force was less busy. The Company countered by saying that there would be no sense of urgency on the part of the shipyard workers if they knew they had all winter to complete the tasks and costs would therefore rise. Except for one ship therefore, that was on "standby" at any given time, the spring refit pattern remained, unaltered.

Captain Whiteway took the ship over from Cammell Laird and on 21st March 1951 her log opened with the ship leaving her builders for the short trip across the Mersey and arriving alongside the Liverpool Landing Stage at 11.04. Next day, she completed her maiden voyage with a round trip from Liverpool to Douglas and back in a moderate, south west gale. After successfully completing her first season, the **Mona's Isle** retired to Barrow on 23rd September.

As with any ship, custom built for her owners' specific services, her career was largely predictable. However, in thirty years' operations some excitement was had and one or two tragedies occurred. 1955 was a year of mixed blessings for the ship. The 8th June 1955 found her in trouble at Fleetwood after she had tried unsuccessfully, to avoid collision with the fishing vessel **Ludo**. The **Ludo** was cut in two and sank with the sad loss of life of one of her men. The **Mona's Isle** put down a boat to help with the rescue, but, trying to render assistance went aground herself and had to go to Cammell Laird's No. 3 dry-dock at Birkenhead for inspection and repairs. The Company's foresight in having a series of five (later six) similar ships, paid good dividends. All the propellers were interchangeable and Cammell Laird kept a spare which would fit any of the sisters. In the event, the **Mona's Isle's** starboard propeller was found to be seriously damaged and was removed and sent to The Manganese Bronze & Brass Company for repair and then retained as the spare. "Owners spare propeller to be transported to the vessel and fitted" was noted in the damage survey report. The ship was out of action for just two days and the total bill was £680.00 (inflation has a lot to answer for these days) including

*The **Mona's Isle** double berthed alongside the car ferry **Ben-my-Chree** at Douglas' Victoria Pier. In their heyday, it was not unusual for four or more ships to tie up, gunwale to gunwale, when pierside berths were at a premium.* Photo: Capt. Westby Kissack.

*A quarter of a century ago! The **Mona's Isle** at Dublin on 30th July 1965. Photo: Richard Danielson collection.*

*The **Mona's Isle** seen from the tug **Union** as she leaves Douglas for the last time on 27th August 1980.   Photo: Richard Danielson.*

shipyard overtime (£79.00) which was justified on the grounds that it saved a further day in dry-dock.

Happier times came later in the season with the ship running two trips from Belfast to Rothesay!

The 1950s and 1960s were still quite exciting times for Steam Packet ships and like Rothesay, other quite unusual places enjoyed Steam Packet sailings from time to time. Some were public and others, private charters. Ayr, for example received several such trips by various Steam Packet ships and Capt. Tom Corteen tells of his visits there and of heart stopping moments having to beat the tide to get over the sand bar. Stranraer, Workington, Whitehaven, Troon and Preston were amongst the **Mona's Isle's** rarer destinations.

For the most part however, the ship operated her owner's complicated "web" of seasonal sailings to the Island from the principal ports and outstations. In 1961, the old landing stage at Fleetwood was found to be unsafe (it had looked that way for quite some time previously) and on 11th September 1961 the **Mona's Isle** arrived there at 21.07 and the route was closed. In fact it was thought that it would be closed permanently as the log sheets carry the poignant comment "last call of a passenger ship to this port". In fact, ten years later on 25th August, the honour again fell to the **Mona's Isle** to re-open the route, after the stage and terminal (wharf was the term always used throughout the log sheets) had been rebuilt.

1964 saw the ship in the worst difficulties she had encountered in her whole career. Her sailing from Liverpool on Friday 14th February had been a stormy one and the ship had sailed to Peel where she lay overnight with the intention of sailing round to Douglas, early the next morning. On Saturday 15th February, having set off at 06.22, within ten minutes the ship had run aground damaging both her propellers, rudder and stern frame. In fact, the divers' report made the blunt statement "Rudder and stern frame gone".

*30th June 1980 dawned wet and grey, but undaunted the **Mona's Isle** operated a Round the Island cruise to commemorate the Steam Packet Company's 150th Anniversary and the launching of her first namesake, a century and a half earlier.*   *Photo: Richard Danielson.*

Local fishing boats towed the ship to a safe anchorage in Peel Bay where she awaited the arrival of the Alexandra Towing Company's steam reciprocating tugs **North End** (1957) and **North Wall** (1959) which were dispatched from Liverpool with all haste. The tow commenced at 22.15 that night and the **Mona's Isle** was safely alongside the Liverpool Landing Stage by 17.43 the next day. Interestingly, even the combined 2;100 horsepower of the two Alexandra tugs was insufficient for the last delicate leg of the manoeuvre and at the Bar Lightship, an additional 980 bhp came to the parties' assistance in the form of the tug **Herculaneum** which helped to steer the stricken vessel up the river. The necessary major repairs were eventually effected in dry-dock but it was not until July that the ship emerged.

The advent of the Steam Packet Company's car ferries gradually meant that the "classic" passenger vessels became redundant. By 1980, the Company's 150th Anniversary, the **Mona's Isle**'s number was up and she was withdrawn that August but not until after she had run a commemorative Round the Island cruise on 30th June to celebrate the sesquicentennial. This then left the technically more advanced **Manxman** (1955), the sixth in the set of which **Mona's Isle** was number five. The **Manxman** soldiered on as the Steam Packet Company's sole classic passenger ship until the end of 1982 when she was sold for static use.

So it was then, that the **Mona's Isle**, the penultimate traditional turbine powered passenger ship, left Manx waters for the last time on 27th August 1980. It was a hazy evening but the weather did not detract from the emotive farewell. At 18.08 she slipped her moorings from the No. 4 berth on Douglas' Victoria Pier and, with her steam whistles proudly blowing, she stormed past the local tug **Union** which, by kind courtesy of her owner and master, Stephen Carter, was a mile or so out especially to witness the event. The **Mona's Isle** set course for Llandudno to return her day-trip passengers.

*Still handsome, even in her last moments, the **Mona's Isle** awaits her Valhalla at the hands of the shipbreakers' cutting torch. She is seen here at Zierikzee, Holland with the Holyhead tug, **Afon Las** (Welsh for Green River) on the left in attendance. Later she was resold to Belgian shipbreakers. Photo: Richard Danielson collection.*

It was then on to Liverpool through the night, where once his faithful old ship was safely berthed at the Landing Stage, Captain Peter Corrin finally rang down "Finished with Engines" at 00.05 on 28th.

Later that day, it was just a short sail across the River to the Morpeth Dock where the ship was laid up to await her fate. Captain Corrin (now the Company's Marine Superintendent) described the events which followed.

"Although she was laid up in the traditional manner, as she had been for so many years before, it was fairly certain that on this occasion she would not remain in Morpeth Dock for very long. As usual at such times, as soon as it was known that she was to be withdrawn from service, rumours abounded as to her future. Plans were discussed for her to be sold for use on the Thames, but the Port of London Authority ruled this out on the grounds that the ship was far too tall to clear London Bridge.

Then came talk that the ship might be sold for use as an oil rig accommodation ship, based at Aberdeen. I recall discussing with my Marine Superintendent, the late Captain Harvey Collister, himself a former master of the vessel, the possibility of me delivering the ship there, should the need arise.

Sadly, nothing came of these plans and on 30th October,

The **Mona's Isle** leaving Douglas at 15.00 on 23rd August 1962, stern first (as was then the practice for all departures) bound for the Scottish harbour of Ardrossan.
Photo: John Shepherd.

the **Mona's Isle** was towed away by the Holyhead tug **Afon Las**, having been sold by the Steam Packet Company to a Dutch Company, for scrap. I believe that she was later resold by Sloop-Berginsbedriyk Van de Marec, Holland, to the well-known Belgian shipbreakers, Van Heygen Freres, who demolished the ship shortly after.

Later that August afternoon, I leaned over the **Mona's Isle's** bridge wing and looked out on the mirror-like River Mersey, towards her birthplace at Cammell Laird's lying just across the water from where she now lay and well within audible distance of her fine sounding steam whistles. The day was calm and still but over the years I had also shared with the old ship, plenty of dirty weather and fog. I reflected on my days in the ship and the many Masters, Officers and Ratings who had served aboard her over the years. I felt privileged that, as she had been my first passenger vessel command, I was honoured to be her last Captain, In some ways, I felt I was repaying years of friendship from a lovely old lady whose time had finally come. No one could have wished for a better ship in which to serve and from a seafarer's viewpoint, she was undeniably the most "Classic" of them all".

P.S. **RYDE**

Built: 1937   *Builder:* Wm. Denny & Bros., Dumbarton.
Speed: 14 knots   *Dimensions:* 223' x 29' (excluding paddleboxes) 52' overall breadth
Gross Tonnage: 603 tons (as built) 566 tons (post war) *Fuel:* Coal
Machinery: Triple expansion three cylinder diagonal engine 1,000 hp
Owners/Operators: Southern Railway Company 1937/1947
   British Transport Commission 1st Jan 1948/1963
   British Railways Board 1963/1969
   British Rail (Shipping and International Services Division) 1969/1970

When the Southern Railway Company came into being on 1st January 1923, it inherited an elderly collection of paddle steamers with which to operate its Portsmouth - Ryde (Isle of Wight) route.

The vessels concerned were all built for the Joint Railway Co's Steam Packet Service - the premier crossing to the island having been worked by the London Brighton and South Coast and the London & South Western Railways in a rare example of co-operation.

The seaborne links to the Isle of Wight were very much integrated with the railway systems and immediately the Southern Railway set out to stamp its mark on what was a badly run-down operation, the island's 56 miles of railway having being operated by no less than three different railway companies.

An immediate order for the **Shanklin** (1924) was followed by the very similar **Merstone** and **Portsdown** (1928), the latter ships representing only part of a massive £2 million investment for the Isle of Wight.

Then in 1930, from Fairfield's of Govan, there appeared the magnificent sisters **Southsea** and **Whippingham**. These two ships were far more modern-looking than anything previously seen at Portsmouth and were mainly built with cruising in mind.

It was then the turn of the **Duchess of Kent** to be replaced and in 1933 she was sold to the New Medway Steam Packet Co. for whom she operated as the **Clacton Queen**. In her place came the **Sandown**, a product of Denny's Dumbarton yard. She was launched in May 1934 and entered service the following month. Although the modern trend in looks continued and she was fitted with a full-width forward observation lounge below the bridge, she retained the typical Portsmouth fully enclosed saloon aft, around the outside of which were alleyways.

Mechanically the **Sandown** was to present a major advance, being the first of the Portsmouth fleet to be fitted with triple-expansion machinery which was more economic in operation and delivered its power far more smoothly. The introduction of the sixth new ship in ten years, during which time the annual number of passengers using the route had risen to well above two million, was fully justified. Only one of the old "Duchesses" still remained but when, on 15th October 1936, the Southern Railway ordered a sister for the **Sandown**, it was apparent that the days of the **Duchess of Norfolk** were numbered. The fact that Messrs. Cosens of Weymouth *(see page 4)* purchased her and, as their **Embassy** she survived until 1967 - an active career of 56 years - speaks volumes for the way in which she was maintained.

*The paddle steamer **Ryde** was the last such vessel to be built for the Portsmouth-Ryde (Isle of Wight) passage. She is seen leaving Ryde Pier during her last season.*
Photo: Andrew Jones.

*The handsome **Ryde** in traditional British Railways colours. Why did they ever change from this fine livery?*   Photo: Havers' Collection.

The new ship building at Dumbarton was duly named **Ryde** and she was launched on St. George's Day (23rd April) 1937. She was in an advanced condition at launch and on the measured mile with 1,066 horsepower showing on the indicator, managed 14.768 knots, which was faster than her sister and in excess of the 14.5 knots contract speed. The **Ryde** cost her owners £46,800 and eventually sailed from Denny's yard on 1st June, arriving at Southampton, where she was handed over, three days later. Although the vessel cost £8,000 more than her sister, she was delivered almost a full month ahead of her contract delivery date.

All Portsmouth - Ryde ships in those days were dual certificated. For the ferry service to Ryde which crossed the relatively sheltered waters of the eastern Solent, a Class IV certificate allowed the **Ryde** to carry 1,050 passengers. When on excursion duties outside the Solent (e.g. round the Isle of Wight) the Class III certificate for 890 came into force. Bunker space for 50 tons of coal made sure that the ship could accomplish these longer day-trips with plenty of fuel to spare.

Accommodation was originally in two classes and remained so until 1951 when, at considerable saving, one class operation was adopted thereby eliminating the need to "double-up" on all aspects of her operation.

At no stage in her career was the **Ryde** identical to her sister. There were always recognition points to which the keen eyed observer could refer, particularly in post war years when the **Sandown**'s forward windows beneath her fo'c'sle were not reinstated. Also, the **Ryde**'s deck house was isolated in order to reduce wind resistance and as a result she was easier to handle than her sister and her gross tonnage was thereby reduced from 603 to 566.

The **Ryde**'s "official" maiden voyage was held over until 1st July 1937 to coincide with the opening of the new all-electric railway service from Waterloo (London) to Portsmouth

On the grid-iron at Newhaven during March 1969. Photo: John Hendy.

Leaving Clarence Pier, Southsea, for Ryde in June 1966. Photo: Norman Bird.

Harbour which sped-up through times from the Island to the capital city. However, the new ship had been in service since mid-June assisting her fleet companions when and where required.

During the war, the **Sandown** and **Ryde** both joined the No.7 Minesweeper Flotilla, the **Ryde** carrying the pennant number J 132. Both ships assisted in Operation Dynamo (the Dunkirk Evacuation) before being converted to Anti-Aircraft ships. The **Ryde** was the first of the Portsmouth vessels back on station after the war, on 7th July 1945. An order for two broad beamed diesel vessels to replace the war losses (**Portsdown** and **Southsea**) saw the revolutionary new **Southsea** and **Brading** in service during the latter part of 1948 by which time the Southern Railway had been nationalised. Fitted with the "magic eye of radar", the new sisters quickly showed their paces, making tremendous savings in fuel and, for the first time ever, giving the Island a lifeline link in all weathers - including fog. Their success was such that in 1951 a third similar ship, the **Shanklin**, appeared on station replacing the paddle steamer of the same name.

The three motor vessels were then to maintain the basic service between Portsmouth and Ryde, the coal-burning paddlers living a seasonal existence, often cruising during the weekdays (particularly to Southampton Docks) or running the secondary Ryde link from Southsea's Clarence and South Parade Piers. Summer Saturdays were hectic when thousands of holiday-makers would arrive and leave the island. Queues many deep would stretch half way down Ryde Pier and as one boat arrived to take up to a thousand away, so they would be replaced by many more, waiting patiently on the pier's wooden decking.

Yet during the late 50's and 60's, holiday trends changed. Cheap holidays to the Continent were becoming available and of those people that still came to the island, increasing numbers used the vehicle ferry from Portsmouth to Fishbourne. The stately, but lumbering, **Whippingham** and the **Sandown** were retired in 1962 and 1965 respectively leaving the **Ryde** as the sole survivor of the once prominent paddle steamer fleet.

It had been the practice for many years to lay-up the **Sandown** and the **Ryde** in the Sussex port of Newhaven. A winter visit there would usually find one of the sisters on the grid, up by the old swing bridge, with other seasonal visitors from Dover nearby.

One of the writers was fortunate enough to manage a delivery trip in the **Ryde** at the start of her 1968 season. On a routine crossing to Ryde, it was difficult to fully appreciate the ship's qualities but on this afternoon "cruise" from Newhaven to Portsmouth, the paddler's undoubted charms were fully realised. She was very much the ferry boat, nowhere on board did one ever feel that one was in the lap of luxury, but her spaciousness both on deck and below made her a vessel which deserved to be explored and that one had to get to know. The other writer, working at Newhaven at the time, recalls the **Ryde** leaving Newhaven for Portsmouth after winter lay-up in the mid 1960's. After steaming into the teeth of a South-westerly all day, the ship's position was noted as being "off Peacehaven" — a distance of about 5 miles having been travelled. Discretion being the better part of valour, the **Ryde** returned to Newhaven to await more clement conditions!

Towards the end of her career, both the Paddle Steamer Preservation Society and the Coastal Cruising Association took her on charters away from her usual haunts: up to Southampton's Royal Pier (of fond memory) and into the western Solent. But perhaps her most adventurous excursion was during September 1968 when Gilbey's Gin chartered her to become their "ambassador" on the Thames, a veritable "floating gin-palace".

When the **Ryde** finally tied-up at Portsmouth Harbour at the conclusion of her 20.30 sailing from Ryde on 13th September 1969, it was truly the end of an era for the service. She remained moored in the harbour at the hulk for a year until it was announced that she had been purchased by the Medway Queen Company for just £12,000. She was removed on the 16th September 1970 and was eventually placed in the former Binfield Millpond adjacent to the famous **Medway Queen**, in a position between East Cowes and Newport on the River Medina.

In preparation for her new role as a "Botel", her boilers were removed (but her engine remains intact) and the after lounge was converted to cabins. Renamed **Ryde Queen**, her opening to the public was marred by heavy rainfall during which water poured through the leaky decks soaking the sleeping customers in their bunks below!

What follows is the ship's sad fall from grace.

Little or no money was spent on her external upkeep and a fire in August 1977 could have ended it all. In her final years, large areas were closed off (including all her decks) and only the forward saloon remained open as a bar. The water had long since disappeared from the old millpond and in 1989, the derelict **Ryde,** now stuck in a sea of mud, closed for business.

The ship was inspected by officers of the Paddle Steamer Preservation Society who announced that over £1 million would be needed to save her. With no work carried out on the ship's hull for over twenty years, any efforts to remove her from her present imprisonment would, in all probability, just as had occurred with the **Medway Queen**, result in her sinking.

As the last survivor of the Southern Railway fleet in England, and the last classic ferry of her type, the **Ryde** deserves better.

*The **Ryde** approaches Southampton's Royal Pier in June 1969. Photo: Nick Robins.*

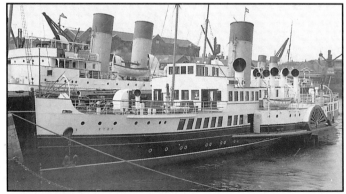

*Newly arrived at Southampton in June 1937, alongside the St. Malo steamer **Dinard**, the **Ryde** looks immaculately turned-out. Photo: John Hendy collection.*

*Twenty years after her imprisonment in Binfield Millpond, Isle of Wight, the derelict **Ryde** closed for business — seemingly a sad end to a fine ship. Photo John Hendy.*

About the previous book in the series.

Book 1, Perfect Bound, 64 pages A5, commences with an introduction to British passenger ship classification and details the various operational limits associated with each class of certificate. This is followed by full text, histories, technical data and many superb, mainly colour photographs of ten favourites: **Lady of Mann** (1976), **Invicta** (1940), **Glen Sannox** (1957), **Free Enterprise I** (1962), **Shepperton Ferry** (1935), **Freshwater** (1959), **Scillonian** (1956), **Caledonia** (1934), **Ben-my-Chree** (1966) and **Royal Iris** (1951).

Supplies of Book 1 are still available to enable readers to complete their sets. See advertisement opposite for full details.

Acknowledgments

The authors would like to express their grateful appreciation to Walter Bowie (himself a dedicated shiplover and photographer who, by profession is the Marketing Officer at Caledonian MacBrayne) for all his help and assistance in making this book a reality. In addition, the authors' good friends Andrew Jones, John Shepherd, David Parsons and Gordon Ditchfield have responded to their pleas by combing their collections for rare material. To them, Ferry Publications partner Miles Cowsill and anyone else who has helped in this endeavour, the authors' extend a wholehearted "thank you".

Also available from

FERRY *Publications*

THE TOWNSEND THORESEN YEARS (2nd Edition)	£6.95
ISLE OF MAN STEAM PACKET (Volume 1)	£1.90
ISLE OF MAN STEAM PACKET (Volume 2 — 2nd Edition)	£4.70
BRITISH CHANNEL ISLAND FERRIES	£1.90
HARWICH — HOOK OF HOLLAND	£3.40
THE VIKING SAGA (Cherbourg & Le Havre 1964-89)	£4.50
ONLY BRITTANY FERRIES	£4.50
P & O EUROPEAN FERRIES — THE FLEET	£1.90
SEALINK ISLE OF WIGHT	£3.40
FERRIES IN CAMERA '90 (full colour)	£5.95
THE MANXMAN STORY	£1.30
FERRY POSTCARDS (SET 2)	£1.90
FANTASIA	£2.95
SALLY LINE	£3.40
EARL WILLIAM	£2.95
SAINT-GERMAIN	£2.95
OLAU	£3.95
FISHGUARD — ROSSLARE	£3.40
THE VERY BEST OF BRITISH (Book 1)	£5.65
BY ROAD — ACROSS THE SEA The History of the Atlantic Steam Navigation Co. Ltd	£8.10
WINSTON CHURCHILL	£2.95

All prices are quoted to include postage and packing within the U.K. For European and Overseas orders please add a further 85p per book.

Send orders to:
    FERRY PUBLICATIONS, 12 MILLFIELDS CLOSE, PENTLEPOIR,
                KILGETTY, DYFED SA68 0SA